Áve grácí

pléua

domínue

ANGELS

A Joyous Celebration

RUNNING PRESS
PHILADELPHIA • LONDON

Library of Congress Cataloging-in-Publication Number
98–68475

ISBN 0-7624-0605-4

This book may be ordered by mail from the publisher.
Please include $1.00 for postage and handling.
But try your bookstore first!

Running Press Book Publishers
125 South Twenty-second Street
Philadelphia, Pennsylvania 19103-4399

Visit us on the web!
www.runningpress.com

Contents

Introduction

A world without angels would be
a world without hope. Angels appear
in the earliest stories of our existence—
winged creatures that belong to a
higher order than man. Angels are
depicted as messengers, musicians,
guardians, cupids, and even warriors.
The angel is a bridge between heaven
and earth, a human form with divine

Angels

alterations—wings, halos, and golden
auras. They are divine messengers
with grace and archetypal beauty or
robust youths with bow and arrow or
harp and flute. Some of the greatest
painters and sculptors in the history
of art have dealt with the image
of the angel. Each artist brought to
his rendering a combination of the
traditional image and a personal

vision. The combination of the unique and the common has produced some of the world's finest works of art.

The Greeks and Romans saw the angel as an allegory for divine wisdom or powers. Statues and frescoes commemorating triumph almost always used a winged figure to represent victory. The winged

Angels

cupid represented the duality
of love; the lovely, playful cherub
wielded a bow and arrow in order
to pierce the heart of his intended.

   With the rise of Christianity
angels became icons of divine
perfection—they were beautiful,
graceful, loyal servants who per-
formed varied services for the
Almighty. They began to inhabit

religious paintings in increasing numbers and in prominent positions. By the early Renaissance, the angel had become a favorite subject in painting, immortalized in the sublime perfection of works by artists such as Botticelli and Raphael.

11

Angels

The art of the post-Renaissance began a slow return to the secular world and its scenes, but angels remained a lasting symbol of the presence of the divine in our earthly realm. Angels continue to inhabit the conscience of our culture. They are not only part of our religious world but also part of our popular literature, myth, and fantasy.

Angels are a reminder to us all of our well-being and serve as inspirations and examples of grace, happiness, and harmony. The more materialistic our world becomes, the more we embrace the idea that angels watch over us and change our lives.

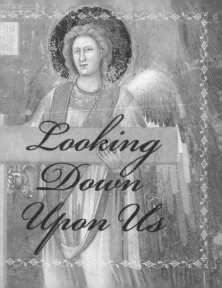

Looking

Down

Upon Us

The guardian angels of life
sometimes fly so high as to be
beyond our sight, but they are
always looking down upon us.

Jean Paul Richter (1763–1825)
French writer and humorist

Looking Down Upon Us

O, beautiful rainbow,
all woven of light!
Heaven surely is open
when thou dost appear
and bending above thee
the angels draw near,
and sing "The rainbow—
the rainbow; the
smile of God is here!"

Sarah J. Hale (1790–1879)
American writer and editor

Angels

Angels are in the heavens,
I am sure, because there are
deeds done by mortals that are
difficult to explain by the mortal
nature of man. The angels of
self-sacrifice and everlasting
devotion, of courage and tender-
ness—they must be fluttering
about in the winds high above,
sometimes taking on
the face of man and his flesh.

Dagobert D. Runes (1902-1982)
American writer

Angels

For God will deign
To visit oft the dwellings
   of just men
Delighted, and with frequent
   intercourse
Thither will send his winged
   messengers
On errands of supernatural grace.

John Milton (1608-1674)
English poet

He shall give his angels

charge over thee,

to keep thee in all thy ways.

Psalm 91:11
The Bible

Angels

The angels . . . regard our safety, undertake our defense, direct our ways, and exercise a constant solicitude that no evil befall us.

John Calvin (1509–1564)
French theologian and reformer

I've heard that little infants
    converse by smiles and signs
With the guardian band of angels
    that round them shines,
Unseen by grosser senses;
    beloved one! dost thou
Smile so upon the heavenly
    friends, and commune with
    them now?

Caroline Anne Southey (1786–1854)
English poet

🐼 Angels

I have seen angels by the sick
    one's pillow;
Their's was the soft tone and
    the soundless tread,
Where smitten hearts were
    drooping like the willow,
They stood 'between the living
    and the dead.'

Unknown

✺ Angels

Four angels to my bed,

Four angels round my head,

One to watch and one to pray

And two to rear my soul away.

Thomas Ady
17th-century English writer

Beside each man who's
   born on earth
A guardian angel takes
   his stand,
To guide him through
   life's mysteries.

Menander of Athens
(c. 343–291 B.C.)
Greek playwright and poet

Angels

When tempted, invoke your angel.
He is more eager to help
you than you are to be helped!
Ignore the devil,
and do not be afraid of him.
He trembles and flees
at your guardian angel's sight.

St. John Bosco (Giovanni Melchior)
(1815–1888)
Italian priest and writer

Angels

There are two angels,
   that attend unseen
Each one of us, and
   in great books record
Our good and evil deeds.
   He who writes down
The good ones, after
   every action, closes
His volume, and ascends
   with it to God,

The other keeps his
    dreadful day-book open
Till sunset, that we may
    repent; which doing,
The record of the action
    fades away,
And leaves a line of white
    across the page.

Henry Wadsworth Longfellow
(1807–1882)
American poet

Angels

When children lay them down
    to sleep,
Two angels come, their watch
    to keep,
Cover them up, safely and warm,
Tenderly shield them from
    harm.
But when they wake at dawn of day,
The two bright angels go away,
Rest from their work of care and love
For God Himself keeps watch above.

Unknown

If there be for him

an angel, an intercessor,

one among a thousand,

to vouch for man's uprightness,

then He is gracious.

Job 33:23
The Bible

Angels

We should pray
to the angels,
for they are given
to us as guardians.

St. Ambrose (c. 340–397)
Italian bishop

Angels

Then, in such hour of need

Of your fainting, dispirited race,

Ye, like angels appear,

Languor is not in your heart,

Weakness is not in your word,

Weariness is not on your brow.

Matthew Arnold (1822–1888)
English poet and critic

Looking Down Upon Us 💀

But Man, proud man,
Dress'd in a little brief authority,
Most ignorant of what he's
   most assur'd,
His glassy essence,
   like an angry ape,
Plays such fantastic tricks
   before high heaven
As makes the angels weep.

William Shakespeare (1564–1616)
English playwright and poet

In this dim world
    of clouding cares,
We rarely know,
    till 'wildered eyes
See white wings
    lessening up the skies,
The angels with us
    unawares.

Gerald Massey (1828–1907)
English poet

Angels

Even the darkest soul passes,

at least once in life, a ray of

awareness of the supernatural,

sometimes at the birth of

a child or the death of a soul.

Dagobert D. Runes (1902–1982)
American writer

And with the morn,
   those angel faces smile
Which I have loved long since,
   and lost awhile.

John Henry Newman (1801–1890)
English cardinal and theologian

Angels

If a man is called to be
a streetsweeper, he should sweep
streets even as Michelangelo
painted, or Beethoven composed
music, or Shakespeare wrote poetry.
He should sweep streets so well that
all the host of heaven and earth
will pause to say, here lived a great
streetsweeper who did his job well.

Martin Luther King, Jr. (1926–1968)
American civil rights leader and minister

He passed the flaming
   bounds of place and time:
The living throne,
   the sapphire-blaze,
Where angels tremble,
   while they gaze,
He saw; but blasted
   with excess of light,
Closed his eyes
   in endless night.

Thomas Gray (1716–1771)
English poet

Angels

Every breath of air and
ray of light and heat,
every beautiful prospect,
is, as it were, the skirts of
their garments, the wav-
ing of the robes of those
whose faces see God.

John Henry Newman (1801–1890)
English cardinal and theologian

Angels . . . with beautiful
wings of silk and crowns
of baby rosebuds . . . all live
together in a castle . . . and
when the angels
want to go some-
place they just
whistle—and
a cloud floats to
the castle door
and picks them up.

And the angels ride through the sky riding the cloud like a magic carpet—under the moon and through the stars— until they're right above us. That's how they can look down and see if we're all right—and sometimes even send messages to us.

From the movie *The Little Princess*

Angels

Unless you can love,
  as the angels may,
With the breath of heaven
  betwixt you. . . .
Oh, never call it loving!

Elizabeth Barrett Browning (1806–1861)
English poet

Love and Compassion

Love's heralds should be thoughts
Which ten times faster glide than
   the sun's beams
Driving back shadows over
   low'ring hills;
Therefore do nimble-pinion'd
   doves draw love;
And therefore hath the wind-swift
   Cupid wings.

William Shakespeare (1564–1616)
English playwright and poet

Angels

Her beautiful hair

dropped over me—

like an angel's wing.

Charles Dickens (1812–1870)
English writer

Angels

LOVE
I imagine the leathery
sound of wings—not bats
but angels lighting down,
naked, gorgeous.

Robert Ferro (1941–1988)

American writer

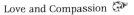

O Lyric love,

Half angel and half bird,

And all a wonder

And a wild desire.

Robert Browning (1812–1889)
English poet

Angels

Stone walls do not a prison make
Nor iron bars a cage;
Minds innocent and quiet take
That for a hermitage;
If I have freedom in my love,
And in soul am free,
Angels alone that soar above
Enjoy such liberty.

Richard Lovelace (1618–1657)
English poet

Self is the only prison that can
  ever find the soul;
Love is the only angel who can
  bid the gates unroll;
And when he comes to call thee,
  arise and follow fast;
His way may lie through darkness,
  but it leads to light at last.

Henry Van Dyke (1822–1891)
American cleric and writer

ANGELS

Angels listen when she speaks: She's my delight, all mankind's wonder. . . .

John Wilmot Rochester (1647–1680)
English poet

Angels

I feel as if it would be flattering an angel to compare such a creature to you. You have been privileged to receive every gift from nature, you have both fortitude and tears.

Victor Hugo (1802–1885)
French writer

She was a phantom of delight
When first she gleamed upon
    my sight;
A lovely apparition . . .
And yet a spirit still and bright,
With something of an angel light.

William Wordsworth (1770–1850)
English poet

Angels

. . . he fell asleep, and dreamed he saw her coming bounding towards him, just as she used to come, with a wreath of jessamine in her hair,

her cheeks bright, and her
eyes radiant with delight; but,
as he looked, she seemed to
rise from the ground; her
cheeks wore a paler hue—her
eyes had a deep, divine radi-
ance, a golden halo seemed
around her head—and she
vanished from his sight. . . .

Harriet Beecher Stowe (1811–1896)

American writer

 Angels

When love speaks,

the voice of all the gods

Makes heaven

drowsy with the harmony.

William Shakespeare (1564–1616)
English playwright and poet

Angels

Of all earthly music that which reaches farthest into heaven is the beating of a truly loving heart.

Henry Ward Beecher (1813–1887)
American cleric

Love and Compassion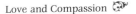

There is music even in the

beauty, and the silent note which

Cupid strikes, far sweeter than

the sound of an instrument.

Thomas Browne (1605–1682)
English physician and writer

Angels

Every saint in heaven is as a flower
in the garden of God, and holy
love is the fragrance and sweet
odor that they all send forth, and
with which they fill the bowers of
that paradise above. Every soul
there is, is a note in some concert
of delightful music, that sweetly
harmonizes with every other note,
and all together blend in
the most rapturous strains. . . .

Jonathan Edwards (1703–1758)
American cleric and theologian

For compassion
a human heart suffices;
but for full and
adequate sympathy with
joy an angel's only.

Samuel Taylor Coleridge (1772–1834)
English poet and critic

Love and Compassion

O welcome, pure-ey'd Faith,

white-handed Hope,

Thou hovering angel,

girt with golden wings!

John Milton (1608–1674)
English poet

Angels

Divine things

must be loved

to be known.

Blaise Pascal (1623–1662)
French scientist and philosopher

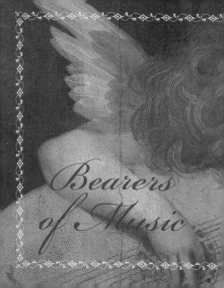

Bearers
of Music

Angels

I want to be an angel,
And with the angels stand,
A crown upon my fore-
   head,
A harp within my hand.

Urania Bailey (1820–1882)
American evangelist and writer

Music soothes us, stirs us up;
it puts noble feelings in us;
it melts us to tears, we know
not how—it is a language
by itself, just as perfect,
in its way, as speech, as words;
just as divine, just as blessed. . . .

Charles Kingsley (1819–1875)
English cleric and writer

MUSIC

Music is well said to be
the speech of angels:
in fact, nothing among
the utterances allowed
to man is felt to be
so divine. It brings us
near to the infinite.

Thomas Carlyle (1795–1881)
Scottish writer and historian

Angels

In Heaven a spirit doth dwell
Whose heart-strings are a lute—
None sing so wild—so well
As the angel Israfel—
And the giddy stars are mute.

Edgar Allan Poe (1809–1949)
American writer and poet

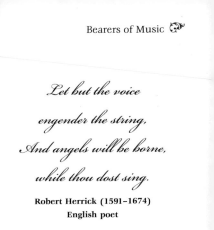

Let but the voice

engender the string,

And angels will be borne,

while thou dost sing.

Robert Herrick (1591–1674)
English poet

Angels

Where the bright seraphim
in burning row
Their loud up-lifted angel
trumpets blow.

John Milton (1608–1674)
English poet

Angels

The angels were all singing out
    of tune,
And hoarse with having little else
    to do,
Excepting to wind up the sun
    and moon
Or curb a runaway young star
    or two.

George Gordon, Lord Byron (1788–1824)
English poet

Whether the angels play only Bach in praising God I am not quite sure; I am sure however, that *en famille* they play Mozart.

Karl Barth (1886–1968)
Swiss theologian and educator

Angels

So is music an asylum.
It takes us out of the actual and
whispers to us dim secrets
that startle our wonder as to who
we are, and for what, whence
and whereto. All the great inter-
rogatories, like questioning angels,
float in on its waves of sound.

Ralph Waldo Emerson (1803–1882)
American writer and poet

O may I join the choir invisible
of those immortal dead who live
again in minds made better
by their presence: live in pulses

stirred to generosity, in deeds
of daring rectitude, in scorn for
miserable aims that end with
self, in thoughts sublime that
pierce the night like stars, and
with their mild persistence urge
man's search to vaster issues.
So to live is heaven; to make the
undying music in the world!

George Eliot (Mary Ann Evans) (1819–1880)
English writer

Angels

. . . Look how the floor of heaven
Is thick inlaid with patinas
   of bright gold:
There's not the smallest orb
   which thou behold'st
But in his motion like an angel
   sings,
Still quiring to the young-ey'd
   cherubins;
Such harmony is in immortal
   souls. . . .

William Shakespeare (1564–1616)
English playwright and poet

Heaven
and Earth

The world has angels all too few,
And heaven is overflowing.

Samuel Taylor Coleridge (1772–1834)
English poet and critic

If God could

make angels,

why did he bother

with men?

Dagobert D. Runes (1902–1982)
American writer

Angels

On the second day,
God created the angels,
with their natural propensity
to good. Later He made beasts
with their animal desires.
But God was pleased with neither.
So He fashioned man,
a combination of angel and beast,
free to follow good or evil.

Midrash Semak
Hebrew biblical text

Angels

There is spiritual life that we
share with the angels of Heaven
and with the divine spirits, for like
them we have been formed
in the image and likeness of God.

Lawrence of Brindisi (1559–1619)
Italian religious leader and writer

Heaven and Earth 🐾

The Earth is to the Sun

What man is to the angels.

Victor Hugo (1802–1885)
French writer

Angels

One of the hardest
lessons we have to learn
in this life . . . is to see
the divine, the celestial,
the pure in the common,
the near at hand—to
see that heaven lies about
us here in this world.

John Burroughs (1837–1921)
American writer and naturalist

Angels

In pride, in reas'ning pride,
    our error lies;
All quit their sphere,
    and rush into the skies!
Pride still is aiming at the
    bless'd abodes,
Men would be Angels,
    Angels would be Gods.
Aspiring to be Gods
    the Angels fell,
Aspiring to be Angels men rebel.

Alexander Pope (1688–1744)
English poet

How fading are the joys
  we dote upon!
Like apparitions seen and gone.
But those which soonest take
  their flight
Are the exquisite and strong—
Like angels' visits,
  short and bright;
Mortality's too weak to bear
  them long.

John Norris (1657–1711)
English philosopher and cleric

Angels

Millions of spiritual creatures walk the earth Unseen, both when we wake and when we sleep.

John Milton (1608~1674)
English poet

Angels

Much on earth is hidden

from us, but to make

up for that we have been

given a precious mystic sense

of our living bond with

the . . . higher heavenly world.

Fyodor Dostoyevsky (1821–1881)
Russian writer

The only thing we are missing
is angels. In this vast world there
is no place for them. And anyway,
would our eyes recognize them?
Perhaps we are surrounded
by angels without knowing it.

Henry Miller (1891–1980)
American writer

Angels

We only live among men,
but there are airy hosts,
blessed spectators,
sympathetic lookers-on,
that see and know and
appreciate our thoughts
and feelings and acts.

Henry Ward Beecher (1813–1887)
American cleric

Outside the open window

The morning air

is all awash with angels.

Richard Purdy Wilbur
American poet

Angels

Outside the doors

of study . . . an angel waits.

Hannah Green
American writer

Angels

Be not forgetful

to entertain strangers,

for thereby some have

entertained angels unawares.

Hebrews 13:2
The Bible

If angels are
entertained unaware,
it is because
they have tact.

Spencer Bayne (1899–1978)
American writer

If some people really see angels where others see only empty space, let them paint the angels. . . .

John Ruskin (1819–1900)
English critic and writer

Angels

I should like to have had
an angelic brush, or forms
of paradise to fashion
the archangel, and to see him
in Heaven, but I have not been
able to rise so high, and in
vain I have searched for him
on earth. So that I have looked
upon that form which I have
established for myself in the Idea.

Guido Reni (1575–1642)
Italian artist

I have been on the verge of being an angel all my life, but it's never happened yet.

Mark Twain (1835–1910)
American writer

Angels

The last thing I should
expect to meet in heaven
would be a dead level
of intellect and taste.
I admire the notion of
some of the theologians
that each individual
angel is a distinct species
in himself.

Joseph Farrell
American academic and writer

Angels

Every man

contemplates an angel

in his future self.

Ralph Waldo Emerson (1803–1882)
American writer and poet

An angel can illumine the
thought and mind of man by
strengthening the power of vision,
and by bringing within his
reach some truth which the angel
himself contemplates.

St. Thomas Aquinas (c. 1225–1274)
Sicilian-born Dominican theologian

The more materialistic
science becomes, the
more angels shall I paint:
their wings are my
protest in favor of the
immortality of the soul.

Edward Coley Burne-Jones (1833–1889)
English artist and designer

*Illustration and
Photography Credits*

National Museum of American Art, Washington D.C./Art Resource, New York: front cover and p. 39 (*Angel*), by Abbott Handerson Thayer.

p. 123 (*Swing Low, Sweet Chariot*), by William H. Johnson.

Scala/Art Resource, New York:

pp. 74–75 (*Music-making Angel*), by Rosso Fiorentino. Uffizi, Florence, Italy.

p. 83 (*The Last Judgement*), detail of angel with trombone, artist unknown. S. Angelo in Formis, Capua, Italy.

back cover and p. 87 (*Angel Playing Violin*), by Melozzo da Forli. Pinacoteca, Vatican Museums, Vatican State.

Victoria & Albert Museum, London / Art Resource, New York:

p. 25 (*The Resurrection, Angel Rolling Away the Stone from the Sepulchre*), by William Blake.

p. 111 (*How Galahad Sought the Sang Real. . .*), by Sir Edward Burne-Jones. Executed in stained glass by William Morris.